疯子与扫把

[美国]迈克·帕尔玛 著
黄运特 译

译林出版社

图书在版编目（CIP）数据

疯子与扫把：汉英对照／（美）迈克·帕尔玛（Michael Palmer）著；黄运特译．—南京：译林出版社，2017.10（2018.4 重印）
（镜中丛书）
书名原文：Madman with Broom
ISBN 978-7-5447-6914-3

Ⅰ.①疯… Ⅱ.①迈… ②黄… Ⅲ.①诗集－美国－现代－汉、英
Ⅳ.①I712.25

中国版本图书馆 CIP 数据核字（2017）第 086654 号

疯子与扫把 ［美国］迈克·帕尔玛／著　黄运特／译

责任编辑　吴莹莹
装帧设计　韦　枫
责任印制　颜　亮

出版发行　译林出版社
地　　址　南京市湖南路 1 号 A 楼
邮　　箱　yilin@yilin.com
网　　址　www.yilin.com
市场热线　025-86633278
排　　版　南京展望文化发展有限公司
印　　刷　恒美印务（广州）有限公司
开　　本　889 毫米 ×1010 毫米　1/32
印　　张　6.625
插　　页　4
版　　次　2017 年 10 月第 1 版　2018 年 4 月第 2 次印刷
书　　号　ISBN 978-7-5447-6914-3
定　　价　58.00 元

“镜中丛书”总序

自2010年起，由我主持的“国际诗人在香港”项目，每年邀请一两位著名的国际诗人，分别与优秀的译者合作，除了举办诗歌工作坊、朗诵会等一系列诗歌活动，更重要的是，由香港牛津大学出版社出版双语对照诗集的丛书。到目前为止，已有八位应邀的国际诗人和译者合作出版了八本诗集，形成了一个小小的传统。这套丛书再从香港到内地，从繁体版到简体版，由译林出版社出版，取名为“镜中丛书”。按原出版时间顺序，包括谷川俊太郎、迈克·帕尔玛、德拉戈莫申科、盖瑞·施耐德、阿多尼斯和特朗斯特罗默的六本诗集。

与此并行的是“香港国际诗歌之夜”——自2009年起创办的香港国际诗歌节，每两年一届。这两个诗歌项目交织互补，为香港提供独特的文化平台，进一步形成汉语诗歌与国际诗歌的双重推动力。

这套丛书的设想基于以下考虑：首先，在国际诗人与汉语译者的文本互动之中，跨越语言的边界；其二，对多语种的译者提出挑战，为丰富现代汉语提供新的品质及方向；其三，在国际诗人、译者和读者之间，在文本对应与参照中，构成某种内在张力，激活一连串语言内外的连锁反应。

这套丛书首先面对的是院校外语专业的大学生，以及初学或精通外语的读者，当然也包括学者、译者和诗人同行。

“镜中丛书”是我和同行合作编辑出版的中英、中法等一系列双语对照诗集丛书的“兄弟姐妹”，共同组成了一个国际诗歌的“大家庭”。诗歌是人类精神家园的保证，也是一个民族苦难中的幸运。

北岛

2015年7月21日

© 克里斯托弗 · 费尔夫

迈克 · 帕尔玛

目录

译者前言

在2005年的一次讲演中，美国著名诗人迈克·帕尔玛曾引用一位苏俄诗人的话宣称："诗歌是一把犁，给时间耕地，把深层的东西翻起来，黑土才会呈现在上面。"从70年代以来，帕尔玛的作品一直以其语言的深度和启示录般的活力，在美国诗坛独树一帜。从最早的《布莱克的牛顿》(1972)到最近即将出版的《线条》，帕尔玛的二十多本诗集既具有英美诗歌传统的优雅，又发挥现代派的大胆创新。融艺术美学、语言哲学和时事政治为一体，深刻挖掘时间与现实，帕尔玛的作品把美国诗歌提到了继60年代垮掉派之后的又一个新高度。

在帕尔玛的字里行间里，我们可以感到诗歌在不断地责问自己，斟酌自己跟世界的关系，寻找自己在现实里的地位。尤其是在人类语言正被鼓吹战争的政客与骗子肆意蹂躏的年代，帕尔玛觉得每一行诗都是一次清洗语言的机会。因此，那些让人产生惰性的陈词滥调，被作者玩于手掌，颠来倒去，点石成金，将它们沦为自己诗歌的笑柄和材料。这一特点使帕尔玛成为美国语言诗派的代表人物之一。

帕尔玛的诗往往不是独白，而是对话；不是独自一人在柏拉图的山洞里给世界发信号，而是在茫茫人海中，在语言的沙漠里寻找回声。他早年的诗集《回音湖札记》，就是探索像蝙蝠一样在黑夜里，靠回音来辨别方向的能力。“他跟谁讲过”、“谁教你不要讲话”、“谁的声音掏空一切”等等，一系列问题，都暗示有一个对话者，一个听众。即便是独白，帕尔玛的叙述者也往往呈现精神分裂症的征兆，“它会说，玫瑰是红的，二二得四——仿佛有人在场”（《循环》）。在世界的黄昏，帕尔玛曾感叹：“我们有幸跟别人一起工作。”他又说，“对话就是思想。”而在对话中，难免有暂时的沉默、尴尬、不安、空缺、犹豫、疑惑、模拟、引用、责问，等等。这些都是帕尔玛作品里常见的场景片断，也是诗歌存在的状态。最可怕的是那“掏空一切”的、独裁暴君式的声音，硬把墙上的有些字“指定为真理”，而另一些作为艺术拍卖（《声明》）。这些“完美的半月”，只是“都市的谎言”（《这个》）。

1996年，在给北岛的英文版诗集《在天涯》所作的序里，帕尔玛提出一个诗歌远近的概念，这同时也是一个时间与世界观的概念。他所谓的 far away near，直译为“遥远的近”，可用中文“远在天边，近在眼前”来理解，说明诗歌所创造的不仅是一个距离观，而且是一种现时性，融合过去与将来。否则，语言将变成威尼斯的那座叹息桥，囚犯经此桥入狱，一去不返，再也看不到外面的世界（《通往语言的路上》）。拒绝历史叙述的单向行驶，拒绝成为僵化语言的囚犯，帕尔玛宣称：“诗歌是对遗忘的反抗。”以这种艺术精神，诗歌才到达一个新的伦理高度，成为对正统文化的抵抗和批判。

黄运特

疯子与扫把

迈克·帕尔玛诗选

Madman with Broom

The realist crows return
at earliest morning.
And the madman with broom,

madman in his nightshirt
with a broom, he too returns.
He thinks to roust the crows

from the mulberry boughs
by jabbing and swirling his broom,
by crazily twirling his broom

in the wet summer air
and hurling curses skyward
beyond the boughs and the crows

towards the fading gods among the fading stars.
But the realist crows know
it is only a man

疯子与扫把

现实主义的乌鸦
一大早回来了。
那疯子拿着扫把，

穿睡衣的疯子
拿着扫把，也回来了。
他想把鸦群

从桑树枝上轰走
用扫把猛刺，急旋，
用扫把疯狂地挥舞

在夏日潮湿的空气里
越过枝杈和鸦群
对天诅咒

咒骂那在消逝的群星间消逝的众神。
可是现实主义的乌鸦知道
那不过是一个人

in a nightshirt after dawn,
that the broom is a broom
and that his cries are nothing more

than words and half-words
the heavy air will swallow.
They rise anyway from the tree

as best to quiet him
and let morning be morning.
Soon enough they'll return again

by twos and threes, settling among
the spreading limbs, their laughter the same
before and after.

在清晨穿着睡衣，
扫把也不过是扫把
他的呐喊也仅仅

是一些词语和半词语
将被沉重的空气吞没。
但它们还是从树上飞起

最好让他安静
让清晨依然是清晨。
很快它们又会回来

三三两两，在伸展的枝杈间
栖息，它们的笑声仍是一样
前后不变。

A Measure

After waking he
waited.

In his mind were
three women.

尺度

醒来后
他等着。

脑中有
三个女人。

Some Eyes

Some eyes are red but dead men
have nothing to say
though they sit up and
talk to you
and their faces turn blue.

某些眼睛

某些眼睛是红的，但死人
无话可说
尽管他们坐起来
跟你聊天
他们脸色发青。

Prose 2

In the game Milford threw a pass to his receiver. He had a game leg but he played. He had a way with the ballgame and was a perfect aim. He threw the ball through the air and it stayed there. It stayed where. It stayed in the cheerleader's yellow hair. It stayed in the 50,000 seat stadium. It stayed in America, on the air.

散文 之二

比赛中米尔福德扔球给
接球员。他腿瘸，可他
还是上了场。他玩球很有一套
招数，扔得准确无误。他
把球扔到空中，它
停在那里。停在哪里。停
在啦啦队员的黄发
里。停在五万人坐席的
体育馆里。停在美国，在
空中。

The End of the Ice Age and Its Witnesses

Yesterday your fever returned
It was near the middle of July

and we went to see the Red King
Then I took out the net

together with the red bird
and put it down

on the bank of the river. Could the
flat milling stone and a

subsistence on seeds be originally
an American invention? We

cuddled on the seat of the car
until she said desperately

I was never unhappier;
then I told them that we wished to

冰川纪的结束及其见证者

昨日你的高烧复发
将近七月中旬

我们去见那位红色国王
然后我拿出网

和红鸟一起
放在

河岸。难道
扁平的磨石和

以种子为食本来
是一项美国发明？我们

在车座上搂抱
直到她迫不及待地说

我从未如此痛苦；
然后我告诉他们，我们希望

continue our journey
because we were not reaching our destination

at all. But the creatures of this island
were very kind. The sky

was a deep green, without clouds
since the rain had been falling regularly

onto the lowest branch of a tamarack
where we hung by our knees. Considering

the look of the trees
we were somewhere in Canada

or the Northeast: flat, blue-green needles
0.8 to 1.3 inches long

that yellow in the fall; ovoid cones,
bark thin, scaly and

gray to reddish brown. The soil
is moist and spongy

继续往前
因为我们根本不会抵达

目的地。可是这个岛上的动物
温和友善。天空

湛绿，万里无云
因为雨一直有规律地

落在一棵松木的矮枝上
在那里我们用膝盖悬挂。从

树的模样来看
我们是在加拿大某地

或是东北：扁平、蓝绿的松针
0.8 至 1.3 英寸长

秋天时发黄；卵形的球果,
薄皮，鳞片

灰色到红褐。车底下
泥土湿润

under the car. E
is white like fog, and A dark,

cycles at some future time
to tell about—

the white tents in the primer
and the kind of flower that trembles easily—

Nothing of the sort is known
or probable on this side of the ocean

nor is there any early record of tents
On a given evening for example

they're playing cards
at the bottom of a swamp or pond; the Tartar

deserts light up; by the stairways
and armchairs of the rocks a

small world, pale and flat
"is coming to understand itself"

软绵绵。E
苍白如雾，A 漆黑，

未来某时的轮回
值得一谈——

初级课本里的白帐篷
和那种轻易颤抖的花——

这些东西在大洋此岸
从未有过，也不可能

也没有关于帐篷的早期记录
某个晚上，比如说

他们在沼泽地
或池塘底下玩牌；鞑靼人的

沙漠灯火通明；在岩石的
阶梯和座椅边上，一个

小小的世界，苍白，平坦
“正开始理解自我”

It Divides ...

It divides into blocks block one

is a stone and the other

block one

is a stone block two

is the third stone

它分成

它分成一块块的，第一块

是一颗石头，另一个

第一块

是一颗石头第二块

是第三颗石头

Sonnet: Now I See Them

Now I see them sitting me before a mirror.
There's noise and laughter. Somebody
mentions that hearing is silver
before we move on to Table One
with the random numbers. I look down
a long street containing numbers.
A white four leans against the fence
and disappears. In the doorway
is the seven, then the x
painted red so you can find it
more easily. Five goes by
without its cap. My father wears
the second x. He was a grey cloud
for a face, and dark lines for arms.

十四行诗：此时我看到

此时我看到他们让我坐在镜子前。
喧闹与笑声。有人
说，听觉是银色
然后我们移到第一张表
全是无规律的数字。我俯视
一条充满数字的长街。
白色的四倚着篱笆
然后消失。站在门道的
是七，然后是 X
漆得鲜红，便于
寻找。五擦身而过
没戴帽子。我爸穿着
第二个 X。他的脸
一团灰云，臂弯两道黑线。

Sonnet: Before We Began

Before we began
you told how the wheel
is getting wider again

A violet wind carries dried flowers
and the cowboy rides
across a dark room

My pen was made in Japan
but the words that come out of it
are made here

in Costa Rica   They spoke to me
about the broken window
These were the "men in blue"

who carry their own windows
wherever they go

十四行诗：我们开始前

我们开始前
你说轮子怎样
又转得更宽

紫色的风携着干燥的花
牛仔在黑暗的
房间里策马而过

我的笔日本制造
而写出来的字
却这里制造

哥斯达黎加　　他们跟我讲
那打破的窗户
这些所谓“蓝衣者”

走到哪里
都扛着自己的窗户

Ninth Symmetrical Poem

(after Southwell)

It's November the thirty-third
of an actual November
and the children sleep in the crystal world
turning their heads from the fire that burns them

The burning children are invisible
but the carriers of wounded thought
are everywhere visible
as letters strung along a word

whose economies
work backward from speech
Mirrored we reflect such things
as they've seen

对称诗 之九

继索斯韦尔[1]

这是一个真实的十一月的
十一月三十三日
孩子们沉睡于水晶世界里
扭头背对那燃烧他们的火焰

燃烧的孩子们隐而不见
可是那些携带伤痕累累的思想的人
却处处可见
像字母串联着一个字

它的意义衍生
是从言语倒退而来
镜子里，我们映现
他们已见过的东西

1　指 16 世纪英国诗人罗伯特 · 索斯韦尔 (Robert Southwell, 1561—1595) 的一首名诗《燃烧的婴儿》(“The Burning Babe”)。

Dance of the Bees (July)

Most people know nothing about polarized light

The scaffold is coming down
and the wind up

but the new silence laws will have a calming effect

Do you remember the winter of the stunned
　　hummingbirds
he asks for the third time, how dogs can

unlearn to chase cats
and cats be taught

to ignore flowering plants
We're moving carefully backward

through the hot weather
Soon it won't quite have begun

蜂舞（七月）

人们对偏振大多一无所知

脚手架塌下来了
风起来了

可是新的消声法令会让一切安宁

你记得蜂鸟被吓呆了的
　　那个冬天吗
他第三次问，怎样让狗

忘记追猫的技术
让猫学会

不理花花草草
我们在炎热的天气里

小心翼翼地倒退
很快炎热就尚未开始

On the Way to Language

The answer was
the sun, the question

of all the fragrances undressed
by the rats in the Pentagon

is Claude's, little
memory jars

empty of their pickled plums
and the tiny

pile of dried bodies under the floorboard
(we had to sell that car)

Summers are always difficult
arriving too soon, too

much wind and the absolute
darkness when it finally descends

通往语言的路上

答案是
太阳，而问题

那有关被五角大楼里的鼠群
驱散的各种香味的问题

是克劳德提出的，小小的
记忆之罐

里面倒空了腌制的李子
车板下面

一小堆干枯的尸体
（我们不得不把车卖掉）

夏日总是困难重重
来得太早，风

太大，当那黑暗
最终降临庄园时

over the plantation. We're not ashamed
of our immense wealth

even somewhat proud
of the cleanliness of the servants' quarters

From the sound of their weeping
they seem happy enough

in their work, childlike
and contrite. The answer was

memory, an efficient
engine driven by earthly

remains and the question
of the valley of desire

crossed by the bridge
of frequent sighs

又是如此彻底。我们并不
以自己的万贯家产为耻

甚至有点
以用人房间的洁净为荣

从他们的哭声里听出
他们似乎安居

乐业，天真烂漫
悔悟自省。答案是

记忆，一台高效率的
引擎由世俗的遗物

操纵，而问题
是有关欲望的峡谷

它上面跨着一座
叹息不止的桥[1]

1 意大利威尼斯市有一座桥，囚犯均过此桥进监狱，此后就看不到外面的世界，因而英国诗人拜伦给它取名“叹息桥”(Bridge of Sighs)。此诗第三段的克劳德指的是法国当代诗人 Claude Royet-Jourenoud (1941—)。

Tenth Symmetrical Poem

A dream in imperfect alexandrines
Through night's eye those tending the book move
as surds or signs, the cooks with their guns
and soldiers with their aprons and copper pots
define arche and telos, passages

translucent as
the old Stalinist says
dolphins in their course, the forest is
hazardous, 'familiar,' its hidden
events. Through night's eye those tending the

book peer out
on a scene from a book
while we who have been translated
(who are waiting to be translated)
do not

对称诗 之十

不完美的英雄体诗中的梦
在黑夜的目光中，那些看守书的人
像无理数或符号一样移动，持枪的厨师
戴着围裙、持着铜锅的士兵
定义了原初和终极，路线

清晰得
像海豚迁移
如那老斯大林主义者曾说的，森林里
危机四伏，“熟悉的”，是其暗藏的
事件。在黑夜的目光中，那些看守书的

人从一本书的场景里
往外窥视
而我们已被翻译的人
（或等着被翻译的人）
却不看

Crossing the Hill

Queens and kings of the perilous edge
of an alphabet we
are are we this
faithful cat crossing the hill

to where time sits
in its midday likeness
or ordinary dark time
like an alphabet

dancing the straight-forward dance
Egypt lives in certain cats
who refuse to scratch
and refuse to sit

here where Egypt lives
as an alphabet
of visible undertakings
mistaken for an actual cat

越过山坡

皇后与国王站在字母
的悬崖边，那就是
我们，难道不是，这只
忠实的猫越过山坡

到那里，时间坐在
它午时的相似里
或寻常的黑暗时光中
像字母

跳着直接的舞步
埃及住在某些猫里
它们拒绝搔痒
拒绝坐在

这里，埃及作为
一套字母活着
一套举止分明的字母
被误认为是一只真实的猫

who is the opposite of an alphabet
geometrical and abstract
and alive because of that
How long will the dry time last

beneath the hill
the serious speakers ask
have the makers unbuilt all this
to decorate a hill

(for A. M.)

一只跟字母相反的猫
像几何图案一样抽象
并因此活蹦乱跳
旱季将持续多久

山坡下
有人严肃地问道
那些创造者把这拆掉
就为了装饰一个山坡？

献给 A. M.

November Talks

Certain faces seem to be ours
pieces of April broken from the main part
window and door entirely ours
who dream of the path of ice
beneath shade, sleep flowering

casually over narrow shoulders
and wheels of a given day within wheels
A headless man is crossing the road
as we remember the earliest shore
outlined by cloud, sleep

wet to our touch, material
of tears offered in sips
so many of us
here, so many missing
who might have been here

(for Bob Perelman)

十一月的谈话

某些面孔似乎属于我们
四月的碎片从整体脱落
窗户与门完全属于我们
梦见阴影下结冰的
小路，睡意在

窄小的肩头随意地开花
某个日子的轮子在大轮子里转动
一个无头人正穿越马路
当我们想起那云霞刻画的
最初的岸，睡意

摸起来湿漉漉的，眼泪般的
液体一小口一小口地斟酌
我们这么多人
在这里，这么多原本可以
在这里的却不见了

献给鲍勃·普尔曼

Notes for Echo Lake 4

Who did he talk to

Did she trust what she saw

Who does the talking

Whose words formed awkward curves

Did the lion finally talk

Did the sleeping lion talk

Did you trust a north window

What made the dog bark

What causes a grey dog to bark

What does the juggler tell us

回音湖札记之四

他跟谁讲过

她信其所见吗

谁在发话

谁的话形成蹩脚的弧线

最后狮子说话了吗

那睡狮说话了吗

你信任朝北的窗户吗

是什么让狗狂叫

是什么使一头灰狗狂叫

魔术师告诉我们什么

What does the juggler's redness tell us

Is she standing in an image

Were they lost in the forest

Were they walking through a forest

Has anything been forgotten

Did you find it in the dark

Is that one of them new atomic-powered wristwatches

Was it called a talking song

Is that an oblong poem

Was poetry the object

Was there once a road here ending at a door

Thus from bridge to bridge we came along

魔术师的脸红告诉我们什么

她站在一个形象里吗

他们在森林中迷了路吗

他们在穿越森林吗

有什么东西忘了吗

你在黑暗里找到它啦

这是那种新型的原子能手表吗

那叫会讲话的歌吗

那是一首椭圆形的诗吗

诗歌曾经是目的吗

这里是否曾有一条路直通到门

就这样我们来了，跨过一座又一座桥

Did the machine seem to talk

Did he read from an empty book

Did the book grow empty in the dark, grey felt hat blowing down the street, arms pumping back and forth, legs slightly bowed

Are there fewer ears than songs

Did he trust a broken window

Did he wake beneath a tree in the recent snow

Whose words formed difficult curves

Have the exaggerations quieted down

The light is lovely on trees which are not large

My logic is all in the melting-pot

My life now is very economical

那机器是否好像在讲话

他是否在读一本空白的书

那书是否在黑暗中变成空白，灰色的毡帽被风吹到大街上，两臂前后伸张，双腿有点罗圈

是否耳朵比歌少

他信任一个打破了的窗户吗

他在最近这场大雪中从一棵树底下醒来吗

谁的话形成复杂的弧线

那些夸夸其谈安静下来了吗

光照在小树上很可爱

我的逻辑都在大熔炉里

我现在的生活很简朴

I can say nothing of my feeling about space

Nothing could be clearer than what you see on this wall

Must we give each one a name

Is it true they all have names

Would it not have been simpler

Would it not have been simpler to begin

Were there ever such buildings

I must remember to mention the trees

I must remember to invent some trees

Who told you these things

Who taught you how to speak

Who taught you not to speak

Whose is the voice that empties

我没法表达自己对空间的感觉

你在这墙上看到的是再清楚不过的了

我们非得给每个都取名吗

他们真的都有名字吗

本来不可以更简单一些吗

这样开始不是可以更简单一些吗

何时有过这样的大楼

我要记得提及那些树

我要记得创造一些树

谁告诉你这些的

谁教你怎样讲话

谁教你不要讲话

谁的声音掏空一切

Song of the Round Man

(for Sarah when she's older)

The round and sad-eyed man puffed cigars as if
he were alive. Gillyflowers
to the left of the apple, purple bells to the right

and a grass-covered hill behind.
I am sad today said the sad-eyed man
for I have locked my head in a Japanese box

and lost the key.
I am sad today he told me
for there are gillyflowers by the apple

and purple bells I cannot see.
Will you look at them for me
he asked, and tell me what you find?

I cannot I replied
for my eyes have grown sugary and dim

圆形人之歌

献给萨拉，等她长大之后

那圆圆的、满目忧伤的人抽着雪茄，仿佛
他还活着。桂竹香
在苹果的左边，紫钟在右边

绿草茵茵的山坡在后面。
我今天很忧伤，满目忧伤的人说
因为我把自己的头锁进日本盒子

钥匙却丢了。
我今天很忧伤，他告诉我
因为苹果旁的桂竹香

和紫钟我都看不见。
你可以帮我看吗，
他问，告诉我你找到什么？

不行，我回答，
因为我烛光下看书太久

from reading too long by candlelight.

Tell me what you've read then
said the round and sad-eyed man.
I cannot I replied

for my memory has grown tired and dim
from looking at things that can't be seen
by any kind of light

and I've locked my head in a Japanese box
and thrown away the key.
Then I am you and you are me

said the sad-eyed man as if alive.
I'll write you in where I should be
between the gillyflowers and the purple bells

and the apple and the hill
and we'll puff cigars from noon till night
as if we were alive.

视线变得模糊不清。

那你跟我讲你读了什么
圆圆的、满目忧伤的人说。
不行，我回答

因为我看太久在任何亮光下
都看不见的东西
我的记忆已疲乏、模糊

而且我把自己的头锁进日本盒子
钥匙扔了。
看来我就是你，你就是我

满目忧伤的人说，仿佛他还活着。
我把你写入我该在的位置
在桂竹香和紫钟之间

苹果和山坡之间
我们从早到晚大抽雪茄
仿佛我们还活着。

So the Dark Figure

So the dark figure falls
backward, arms out and
eyes wide, through the purple

door to another
world. No hint had
been given him

that he would be called
upon and taken
into this painting

(for Bruce McGaw)

这样，那黑影

这样，那黑影往后
倒下，双臂张开
两眼睁大，穿过紫色的

门，到另一个
世界。没有人
曾提醒他

他会被召唤
并带进
这幅画里

献给布鲁斯·麦克高

Dearest Reader

He painted the mountain over and over again
from his place in the cave, agape
at the light, its absence, the mantled
skull with blue-tinted hollows, wren-
like bird plucking berries from the fire
her hair alight and so on
lemon grass in café in clear glass.
Dearest reader there were trees
formed of wire, broad entryways
beneath balconies beneath spires
youthful head come to rest in meadow
beside bend in gravel road, still
body of milky liquid
her hair alight and so on
successive halls, flowered carpets and doors
or the photograph of nothing but pigeons
and grackles by the shadow of a fountain.

最亲爱的读者

居于洞里，他把山
画了一遍又一遍，目瞪口呆
对着光，它的消失，披着斗篷的
骷髅眼眶里发蓝，鹪鹩般的
鸟从火中啄取浆果
她的秀发轻飘，如此等等
咖啡馆的柠檬草装在透明杯里。
最亲爱的读者，有些树
是铁丝做成的，宽敞的入口
在阳台下，在塔尖下
年轻的头靠在草坪上
那碎石路拐角处，静止的
身躯如乳色液体
她的秀发轻飘，如此等等
间间相延的厅堂，花纹地毯，门
或空白的照片，里面只有鸽子
和鹩哥在喷泉的影子旁。

All Those Words

All those words we once used for things but have now discarded in order to come to know things. There in the mountains I discovered the last tree or the letter A. What it said to me was brief, "I am surrounded by the uselessness of blue falling away on all sides into fields of bitter wormwood, all-heal and centaury. If you crush one of these herbs between your fingers the scent will cling to your hand but its particles will be quite invisible. This is a language you cannot understand." Dismantling the beams of the letter tree I carried them one by one down the slope to our house and added them to the fire. Later over the coals we grilled red mullets flavored with oil, pepper, salt and wild oregano.

那一切词语

那一切词语我们曾用来代替事物，而现在都抛弃了，以便我们认识事物。在山里我找到最后一棵树或字母A。它跟我讲的话很简短："围绕我的是毫无用处的蓝色，纷纷从苦艾、百灵草和矢车菊的野地里消逝。假如你用指头把其中一种草药弄碎，那气味就会沾在你手上，可是它的颗粒很难看到。这是一种你无法理解的语言。"我把字母树的枝干折断，然后一根根地扛下山，到我们的房子，扔到火里。后来在火炭上我们烧烤用油、胡椒、盐和野牛至调味过的红鲣鱼。

The Village of Reason

This is a glove
or a book from a book club

This is the sun
or a layer of mud

This is Monday,
this an altered word

This is the village of reason
and this an eye torn out

This is the father
or a number on a chart

This is a substitute,
this the thing you are

This is the varnished picture
or else an accepted response

理性的村庄

这是一只手套
或一本图书俱乐部的书

这是太阳
或一层淤泥

这是周一，
而这，一个改写的字

这是理性的村庄
而这，一只抠出的眼睛

这是父亲
或图表上的一个数字

这是代替物，
这，就是你

这是一张美化过的照片
不然就是一个被接受的答复

This is the door

and this the word for door

This is a reflex caused by falling

and this a prisoner with an orange

This is a name you know

and this is the poison to make you well

This is the mechanism

and this the shadow of a bridge

This is a curve

and this its thirst

This is Monday,

this her damaged word

This is the trace

and this the term unmarked

This is the sonnet

and this its burning house

这是门
而这，门的字

这是摔倒时的条件反射
而这，一名囚犯拿着一颗橘子

这是一个你知道的名字
而这是让你康复的毒药

这是机械
而这，桥的影子

这是一条曲线
而这，它的渴望

这是周一，
这，她那损伤的字

这是痕迹
而这，未标记的术语

这是十四行诗
而这，它那燃烧的房子

You are in this play

You are its landscape

This is an assumption

the length of an arm

This is a poppy,

this an epilogue

你在这场戏里
你是它的布景

这是一个假设
长约一只手臂

这是一朵罂粟花，
这，一篇后记

This Time

(another for Sarah)

Once I fell in the ocean when

I didn't know I fell in the ocean

Then Momma got me out

This isn't true

only something I remember

Once in the park I broke in half

and lost one half

which half I don't remember

Once I was in a room

It grew larger and larger

why I don't remember

One time I turned blue all over

这次

再献给萨拉

有一次我掉进海里
当我不知道自己掉进海里时

然后妈妈把我捞上来
这不是真事

只是我这样记得
有一次在公园我摔成两半

丢了一半
哪一半我忘了

有一次我在一个房间里
它变得越来越大

为什么我忘了
有一次我全身发蓝

then got clear as glass
This really happened

but not to me
Once I couldn't see

for a while
so I listened lying down

Another time I looked out the window
and saw myself at the window

across the street
This time it was me

然后透明得像玻璃

这事真的发生过

只是不是我

有一次我暂时

失明

就躺下聆听

另一次我在窗口眺望

看到自己在窗外

穿过大街

这次真的是我

Fifth Prose

Because I'm writing about the snow not the sentence
Because there is a card—a visitor's card—and on that
card there are words of ours arranged in a row

and on those words we have written house, we have
written leave this house, we
have written be this house, the spiral of a house,
channels through this house

and we have written *The Provinces* and *The Reversal*
and something called the *Human Poems*
though we live in a valley on the Hill of Ghosts

Still for many days the rain will continue to fall
A voice will say Father I am burning

Father I've removed a stone from a wall, erased a
picture from that wall,
a picture of ships—cloud ships—pressing toward the
sea

散文之五

因为我描写的是雪，不是句子
因为有一张卡片——一张来客的卡片——在那上面我
　　们的文字排成一行

在那些字上我们写房子，我们写
　　离开这房子，我们
写成为这房子，房子的转梯，穿过
　　房子的通道

我们写了《省区》和《反转》，以及
　　所谓的《人类诗》
尽管我们住在鬼山的幽谷里

雨依然会连下很多天
一个声音会说：主呵，我在燃烧

主呵，我从墙上挖出一块石头，从那墙上
　　抹掉一幅画，
一幅船的画——云舟——逼近大海

words only
taken limb by limb apart

Because we are not alive not alone
but ordinary extracts from the tablets

Hassan the Arab and his wife
who did vaulting and balancing

Coleman and Burgess, and Adele Newsome
pitched among the spectators one night

Lizzie Keys
and Fred who fell from the trapeze

into the sawdust
and wasn't hurt at all

and Jacob Hall the rope-dancer
Little Sandy and Sam Sault

Because there is a literal shore, a letter that's blood-red

只有文字
被一一肢解

因为我们并不活着，也不孤单
只是出自书板的普通引文

阿拉伯人哈杉和他的妻子
表演撑竿跳与平衡术

科尔曼和伯吉斯，还有阿黛尔·纽森姆
一天晚上安排在观众中间

莉齐·凯斯
和弗雷德从秋千上摔下

掉进锯末堆
却不伤毫毛

走钢索的雅各布·霍尔
小桑迪和山姆·索尔特[1]

因为确实有一个河岸，一个血红的字母

1　这些均为一个 19 世纪马戏团的表演者。

Because in this dialect the eyes are crossed or quartz

seeing swimmer and seeing rock
statue then shadow

and here in the lake
first a razor then a fact

因为在这个方言里眼睛不是斗鸡就是石英

看见游泳者，看见石头
塑像，然后影子

而在这湖里
先是剃刀，然后是事实

From "Baudelaire Series"

A man undergoes pain sitting at a piano
knowing thousands will die while he is playing

He has two thoughts about this
If he should stop they would be free of pain

If he could get the notes right he would be free of pain
In the second case the first thought would be erased

causing pain

It is this instance of playing

he would say to himself
my eyes have grown hollow like yours

my head is enlarged
though empty of thought

Such thoughts destroy music
and this at least is good

波德莱尔系列（选一）

一个人坐在钢琴前感受痛苦
深知成千上万的人会在他演奏时死去

对此他有两个想法
假如他停下，他们将会摆脱痛苦

假如他弹对了，他将会摆脱痛苦
后者会使前者无效

于是引起痛楚

正是在这弹琴的一刻

他会对自己说
我的双眼已变得跟你一样地空洞

我的脑袋膨胀
尽管空如废囊

这些想法破坏音乐
这至少还是好事

Sun

Write this. We have burned all their villages

Write this. We have burned all the villages and the people in them

Write this. We have adopted their customs and their manner of dress

Write this. A word may be shaped like a bed, a basket of tears or an X

In the notebook it says, It is the time of mutations, laughter at jokes, secrets beyond the boundaries of speech

I now turn to my use of suffixes and punctuation, closing Mr. Circle with a single stroke, tearing the canvas from its wall, joined to her, experiencing the same thoughts at the same moment, inscribing them on a loquat leaf

太阳

这样写。我们烧毁了他们所有的村庄

这样写。我们烧毁了所有的村庄和里面的人

这样写。我们接受了他们的习俗和穿着方式

这样写。一个字可写成像一张床、一篮子眼泪或一个 X

笔记本里说，这是突变的时代，听笑话开怀大笑，言语的界外暗藏机密

我现在开始注意自己后缀和标点的用法，一笔完成圆圈先生，把画布从墙上撕下，跟她一起，同时感受同样的想法，把它们刻写在枇杷叶上

Write this. We have begun to have bodies, a now here and a now gone, a past long ago and one still to come

Let go of me for I have died and am in a novel and was a lyric poet, certainly, who attracted crowds to mountaintops. For a nickel I will appear from this box. For a dollar I will have text with you and answer three questions

First question. We entered the forest, followed its winding paths, and emerged blind

Second question. My townhouse, of the Jugendstil, lies by Darmstadt

Third question. He knows he will wake from this dream, conducted in the mother-tongue

Third question. He knows his breathing organs are manipulated by God, so that he is compelled to scream

Third question. I will converse with no one on those

这样写。我们开始拥有肉体，一个此刻还在这里，一个此刻已经离去，一个过去消逝已久，一个过去尚未到来

放我走吧，因为我已死了，我正在一本小说里，我曾是一位抒情诗人，当然，能吸引众人到山顶。给我五分钱，我就从这个箱子里现形。给我一块钱，我就跟你谈文本，回答三个问题

第一个问题。我们走进森林，沿着蜿蜒的小道，蒙着眼睛出来

第二个问题。我的住宅，新艺术风格的，位于达穆斯塔特旁边

第三个问题。他知道他会从这个梦里醒来，这个用母语做的梦

第三个问题。他知道他的呼吸器官是被上帝操纵，因而他被迫大声尖叫

第三个问题。每周以Y结尾日子里，我不跟任何人

days of the week which end in y

Write this. There is pleasure and pain and there are marks and signs. A word may be shaped like a fig or a pig, an effigy or an egg

but

there is only time for fasting and desire, device and design, there is only time to swerve without limbs, organs or face into a

scientific

silence, pinhole of light

say this. I was born on an island among the dead. I learned language on this island but did not speak on this island. I am writing to you from this island. I am writing to the dancers from this island. The writers do not dance on this island

Say this. There is a sentence in my mouth, there is a chariot in my mouth. There is a ladder. There is a lamp whose light fills empty space and a space which swallows light

A word is beside itself. Here the poem is called *What Speaking Means to Say*

谈话[1]

这样写。有欢乐与痛苦，有标记与符号。一个字可写成像无花果或猪，像肖像或鸡蛋

但是

仅有时间来绝食与渴望，设计与谋划，仅有时间来急转弯，尽管没有四肢、器官或脸，进入

科幻的

沉寂，透光的针眼

这样说。我在一个岛屿的死人群里出生。我在这个岛上学会语言却没在这个岛上说话。我正从这个岛上给你写信。我正给这个岛上的舞蹈者写信。在这个岛上，作者不跳舞

这样说。我嘴里有一个句子，我嘴里有一辆战车。有一架梯子。有一盏灯，它的亮光填满空间，有一个空间吞噬亮光

一个字身不由己。这首诗题为《言语想说

的话》

1　英文里一星期的七个日子都是用字母 y 结尾的。下文“罐子平原”、“芦苇平原”，以及“乃良”均为越战期间被美军狂轰滥炸过的柬埔寨地点。

though I have no memory of my name

Here the poem is called *Theory of the Real,* its name is *Let's Call This,* and its name is called *A Wooden Stick*. It goes yes-yes, no-no. It goes one and one

I have been writing a book, not in my native language, about violins and smoke, lines and dots, free to speak and become the things we speak,

pages which sit up, look around and row resolutely toward the setting sun

Pages torn from their spines and added to the pyre, so that they will resemble thought

Pages which accept no ink

Pages we've never seen—first called *Narrow Street,* then *Half a Fragment, Plain of Jars* or *Plain of Reeds,* taking each syllable into her mouth, shifting position and passing it to him

Let me say this. Neak Luong is a blur. It is Tuesday

尽管我记不得自己的名字

这首诗题为《真实理论》，其名为《我们叫它这个》，其名为《木棍》。诗云：是是非非。诗云：一个接一个

我一直在写一本书，不用我的母语，有关小提琴和烟雾，线和点，畅所欲言和说啥就变成啥，

坐起来的书页，环顾四周，朝着落日执着地荡桨

从书脊上撕下篇页，加到火葬堆里，以便它们能形如思想

不接受墨水的书页

我们从未见过的书页——先是题为《窄街》，然后叫《半个碎片》，《罐子平原》或《芦苇平原》，她把音节逐个放到嘴里，更换位置，传递给他

让我说。乃良已一片模糊。在阔叶森林里今天是星期

in the hardwood forest. I am a visitor here, with a notebook

The notebook lists My New Words and Flag above White. It claims to have no inside

only characters like A-Against-Herself, B, C, L and N, Sam, Hans Magnus, T. Sphere, all speaking in the dark with their hands

G for Gramsci or Goebbels, blue hills, cities, cities with hills, modern and at the edge of time

F for alphabet, Z for A, an H in an arbor, shadow, silent wreckage, W or M among stars

What last. Lapwing. Tesseract. X perhaps for X. The villages are known as These Letters—humid, sunless. The writing occurs on their walls

二。这里我是来客，带着一个笔记本

笔记本里列着“我的新词”和“白色上的旗帜”。它宣称没有内容

只是一些角色，如跟她自己作对的 A，B，C，L 和 N，山姆，汉斯·玛格努斯，T. 斯菲尔，都在黑暗中用手比画着讲话

G 代表格拉姆西或戈贝尔，青山，城市，有山的城市，摩登，站在时间的边缘

F 代表字母表，Z 代表 A，一个 H 在凉棚下，影子里，沉寂的废墟，W 或 M 在群星间

最后是什么。田凫。镶嵌物。X 或许代表 X。那些村庄名叫“这些字母”——湿热，无日。文字写在它们的墙上

Construction of the Museum

In the hole we found beside the road
something would eventually go

Names we saw spelled backward there

In the sand we found a tablet

In the hole caused by bombs
which are smart we might find a hand

It is the writing hand
hand which dreams a hole

to the left and the right of each hand

The hand is called day-inside-night
because of the colored fragments which it holds

We never say the word desert
nor does the sand pass through the fingers

博物馆的建造

我们在路边找到的洞
最终会有东西进去

我们看到的名字在那里都是倒写

在沙里我们找到一块书板

在灵敏炸弹轰出来的洞里
我们或许会找到一只手

它是一只写字的手
它梦见一个洞

在每只手的左右

那手名叫“黑夜中的白昼”
因为它握着多彩的碎片

我们从不说沙漠这个词
沙也不从手指间流过

of this hand we forget

is ours

We might say, Memory has made its selection,

and think of the body now as an altered body

framed by flaming wells or walls

What a noise the words make

writing themselves

(for E. H., 11 apr 91)

在这只我们已忘记
是自己的手上

我们或许会说，记忆已作出选择，
把现在的身躯想成已改变的身躯
以燃烧的井或墙为框架

那些字喧哗不已
书写自己

献给 *E. H.*，*1991* 年 *4* 月 *11* 日

Recursus

The voice, because of its austerity, will often cause dust to rise.

The voice, because of its austerity, will sometimes attempt the representation of dust.

Someone will say, I can't breathe—as if choking on dust.

The voice ages with the body.

It will say, I was shaped by light escaping from a keyhole.

Or, I am the shape of that light.

It will say, For the body to breathe, a layer must be peeled away.

It will say, What follows is a picture of how things are for me now.

循环

那声音，由于它的严厉，经常会惹起尘埃。

那声音，由于它的严厉，有时会企图模拟尘埃。

有人会说，我透不过气——仿佛被尘埃窒息。

声音随着肉体衰老。

它会说，锁眼里逃出来的光塑造了我的形状。

或者，我就是那光的形状。

它会说，身体要呼吸，就得剥掉一层。

它会说，接下来是一张图片，代表我此时的处境。

It will say, The rose is red, twice two is four—as if another were present.

The dust rises in spirals.

It will say, The distance from Cairo to anywhere is not that great.

As if one had altered the adjustment of a microscope.

Or examined its working parts.

Possibly an instrument covered with dust and forgotten on a shelf.

Beside a hatbox and a pair of weathered boots.

The voice will expand to fill a given space.

As if to say, This space is not immeasurable.

This space is not immeasurable.

When held before your eyes.

它会说，玫瑰是红的，二二得四——仿佛有人在场。

尘埃盘旋而起。

它会说，从开罗到哪里都不太远。

仿佛有人调整了显微镜的刻度。

或检查过它的部件。

可能是一架仪器盖满尘埃，遗忘在架子上。

在一个帽子盒与一双破靴子旁边。

那声音会扩张，充满指定的空间。

仿佛说，这空间并非不可测量。

这空间并非不可测量。

当它摆在你的眼前。

And which voice is it says (or claims to say), Last night I dreamt of walls and courses of brick, last night I dreamt of limbs.

As you dream—always unwillingly—of a writing not visible and voices muffled by walls.

As if the question: lovers, prisoners, visitors.

The voice, as an act of discipline or play, will imitate other voices.

This is what I am doing now.

This is what I'm doing now.

The clock behind my back, its Fusée mechanism.

Voice one recognizes from years before.

Beneath water, hidden by a spark.

Here at the heart of winter, or let's say spring.

Voice with a history before its eyes.

哪个声音说（或宣称要说），昨晚我梦见墙与砖头的纹路，昨晚我梦见肢体。

当你梦到——总是身不由己——看不见的文字和被墙压抑的声音。

仿佛那些问题：情人，囚犯，来客。

那声音，作为训练或游戏，会模拟别的声音。

这是我此时正在干的。

这是我此时正干的。

我背后的钟，是均力圆锥轮装置。

多年前熟悉的声音。

在水下，藏在亮光里。

这里，冬天的深处，或者说春天。

声音，它的眼前有一段历史。

With a blue dot before its eyes.

History of dust before its eyes.

It will say, as if remembering, The letter S stands for
a slow match burning.

On the table before me.

No numbers on this watch.

And I live in a red house that once was brown.

A paper house, sort of falling down.

Such is the history of this house.

It looks like this.

Looks just like this.

We think to say in some language.

(to Porta)

眼前有一个蓝点。

眼前有尘埃的历史。

它会说，仿佛在回忆，字母 S 代表一根慢慢燃烧的火柴。

在我前面的桌子上。

这块手表上没有数字。

我住的红房子曾经是褐色的。

一座纸房子，有点东倒西歪。

这就是这座房子的历史。

它看上去如此。

看上去就是如此。

我们考虑用某种语言说。

献给波塔

Disclosures

1

Beneath the writing on the wall
is the writing it was designed

to obscure. The two together
form a third kind

2

There is no writing
on the wall's other side

Perhaps this lack
constitutes a fourth kind

3

Some of the writing on the wall
will be designated as truth

声明

1

墙头的字下面
是它蓄意掩盖的

另一些字。两者一起
构成第三种字。

2

墙的另一面
没有文字

或许这空缺
算是第四种字

3

墙上有些字
将会被指定为真理

some as art

4

It is said to represent a mirror
of everyday life in its time

5

“Fabius Naso
talks through his asshole

and shits out his mouth”
for example

6

“Foute les Arabes”
for example

7

Certain words and images

有些为艺术

4

据说它代表一面镜子
反映当时的日常生活

5

比如说
"法比尔斯·纳索

从屁眼讲话
用嘴巴拉屎"

6

比如说
"操阿拉伯人"

7

有些字和图像

or parts of images

have been chipped away
These often turn up for sale

at sidewalk stalls
before the walls

of other cities

8

I too have an image for sale
It's the image of a poem

and is to be found
on the reverse of this sheet

或图像的一部分

已被人凿掉
它们往往

在别的城市
城墙前的路边小摊

被拍卖

8

我也有一个图像要卖
是一首诗的图像

在这张纸的背后
你能找到它

Far Away Near

"We link too many things together."

Agnes Rouzier

As it's said in *The Fragments*
I met the blind typist

inventor of words
The iris of the eye

is an inverted flower
and the essay on snow

offers no beginning
only an aspect of light

beneath a gate
only a photograph of earth

远在天边，近在眼前[1]

我们把太多东西联系在一起了。

阿格尼丝 · 罗泽尔

正如《断篇》里说的
我遇到那位盲人打字员

造字的人
眼球的虹膜

是一朵倒挂的花
那篇关于雪的文章

没有提供开头
只有一个光的侧面

在门下
只有一张大地的照片

1 英文原文为“far away near”，直译是“遥远的近”。详见“译者前言”。

only a fold

a grammar reciting its laws

Just as the clatter

seems distant

and dies without further thought

that moment we ask

Have we reached the center yet, or

Should there be more blue do you think

or just a different shade of blue

all the while tacitly acknowledging

that by blue

she might have meant red

and by red ...

As it's said

we must train our guns toward the future

where the essay on light will obviate time

只有一个折面
一套语法在吟诵自己的规则

正当那咔嗒咔嗒声
显得很遥远

毫无顾虑地消逝
在那一刻我们间

我们到达中央了吗，或者
你觉得要不要再添一点蓝色

还是用不同深度的蓝色
在这同时，我们默认

她指的蓝色
有可能是红色

而她指的红色……
常言道

我们必须把枪对准未来
在那里关于光的文章将逃遁时间

and the essay on smoke
will cause the ground to open

One day I completed the final word
of a letter to my father

in what key I forget
After the ink had dried

I noticed the rain lit by a streetlamp
shaped like a conical hat

I noticed the map
of the moon you had left

half in shadow on my desk
In a city near the North Sea

white nights passed as I read
of an aviator downed

in the Barr Adjam
during the war directly after

而关于烟的文章
将使大地开裂

有一天我写完
给父亲的信的最后一个字

用什么音调我却忘了
当墨迹干后

我注意到雨被街灯
照亮成尖顶帽的形状

我注意到你留下的
月亮的地图

半遮半掩在我的书桌上
在北海边上的一个城市

白夜消逝时，我在读
一个在巴尔-阿加姆被打下来的

飞行员的故事
在战时，紧跟在那场

the war to end all wars

sightless and burned across

three-fourths of his body

Listening in twin silences

his name had disappeared

from his lips

As it's said in The Fragments

There once was a language with two words

and the picture of an apple tree

As it's said

The ravens present a paradox

We learn a new gesture

utter unintelligible sounds

in a cheerful voice perhaps

pointing to the sky

where the rain continues

终结一切战争的战争之后
双目失明，全身烧伤

四分之三
在双重的静寂里聆听

他的名字
已从唇边消失

正如《断篇》里说的
曾有一种语言只含两个字

再加一幅苹果树的画
常言道

乌鸦成为一个悖论
我们学习一种新手势

嘟哝一些模糊的声音
或许以一种快活的语气

指向天空
那里雨还在继续

Autobiography 3

Yes, I was born on the street known as Glass—as
Paper, Scissors or Rock.

Several of my ancestors had no hands.

Several of my ancestors used their pens

in odd ways.

A child of seven I prayed for breath.

Each day I passed through the mirrored X

into droplets of rain congealed around dust.

I never regretted this situation.

Though patient as an alchemist I failed to learn English.

Twenty years later I burned all my furniture.

自传之三

是的，我出生在一条叫玻璃的街道上——也叫石头、剪刀，或布。

我的几位祖先没有手。

我的几位祖先握笔的样子

很怪。

七岁时我为呼吸祈祷。

每天我穿过镜中的 X 进入尘埃上凝固的雨点。

我对此从未反悔。

尽管我有炼金术士般的耐性，却还是没学会英文。

二十年后我把所有的家具都烧了。

Likewise the beams of my house

to fuel the furnace.

Once I bought an old boat.

I abandoned the tyrannical book of my dreams

and wrote about dresses, jewels, furniture and menus

eight or ten times in a book of dreams.

It sets me to dreaming when I dust it off.

Our time is a between time; best to stay out of it.

Send an occasional visiting card to eternity or a few
stanzas to the living

so they won't suspect we know they don't exist.

Sign them Sincerely Yours, Warmest Regards,
Thinking of You or Deepest Regrets.

我家房子的栋梁

也当成锅炉的燃料。

有一次我买了一条旧船。

我放弃了暴君似的梦幻之书

改成去写服装、珠宝、家具和菜单

八遍或十遍地写，在梦幻之书里。

当我拂去尘埃，它就引我入梦。

我们的时间是过渡时间；不宜待在里面。

偶尔给永恒寄一张问候卡或给生者寄几行诗

以免他们怀疑我们知道他们并不存在。

签名处写“您最真诚的”、“深切问候”、“想念您”或
“无比悲哀”。

Brown river outside my window, an old boat riding the current.

What I like most is to stay in my apartment.

So that is my life, pared of anecdotes.

I go out occasionally to look at a dance.

Otherwise the usual joys, worries and inner mourning.

Occasionally in an old boat I navigate the river

when I find the time.

Water swallows the days.

I think maybe that's all.

I have to say

except that an irregular heart sometimes speaks to me.

我的窗外是一条褐色的河流，一艘老船在乘风破浪。

我最喜欢的是待在自己的房间里。

那就是我的生活，除却逸事之后。

我偶尔出去看跳舞。

不然只有日常的乐趣、忧虑和内心的悲哀。

偶尔我开一条老船在河上巡航

当我有空时。

水把日子吞没。

我想我要讲的可能就这么多

除了一颗跳速不齐的心有时会跟我说话。

It says, A candle is consuming a children's alphabet.

It says, Attend to each detail of the future-past.

Last night the moon was divided precisely in half.

Today a terrifying wind.

它说，蜡烛在燃烧孩子们的字母表。

它说，注意未来 / 过去的每个细节。[1]

昨夜，月亮被对半平分。

今天，一场可怕的风。

1 原文 future-past（未来 / 过去）代表作者把未来与过去混在一起，创造诗歌现时的时间观。

Study

In a darkened room they
speak as one against the
religion of the word, against
the prophetic, the sublime, the
orphic call. It is a
strange conversation, coming as it
does after hours of making
love, mid-afternoon till now, at
this their second meeting, shutters
closed to block the lamplight
outside. Seated on the bed,
the curve of her back
toward him, she is smoking.
It is unclear whether they
believe what they are saying.

练笔

在黑暗的房间里他们
异口同声地反对
文字宗教，反对
预言、崇高，以及
俄耳甫斯的召唤。这是一次
奇怪的交谈，尤其是
做爱好几个小时
之后，从下午到现在，他们的
第二次约会，紧闭的
百叶窗挡住了外面的
街灯。端坐床上，
她后背的弧线
冲着他，她在吸烟。
很难说他们是否
相信自己在讲的话。

I Do Not

Je ne sais pas l'anglais.

Georges Hugnet

I do not know English.

I do not know English, and therefore I can have nothing to say about this latest war, flowering through a nightscope in the evening sky.

I do not know English and therefore, when hungry, can do no more than point repeatedly to my mouth.

Yet such a gesture might be taken to mean any number of things.

I do not know English and therefore cannot seek the requisite permissions, as outlined in the recent protocol.

Such as: May I utter a term of endearment; may I now

我不

我不懂英文。

乔治 · 休格纳

我不懂英文。

我不懂英文，所以我对最近的战争
那在夜视镜的晚空开花的战争
无话可说。

我不懂英文，所以当我饥饿时，只能
对着自己的嘴巴不断比画。

但是这样的手势可作多种阐释。

我不懂英文，所以无法申请必要的
准许，如最新条令里陈述的。

比如说：我可以说一句亲热的话吗；我可以

proceed to put my arm or arms around you and apply gentle pressure; may I now kiss you directly on the lips; now on the left tendon of the neck; now on the nipple of each breast? And so on.

Would not in any case be able to decipher her response.

I do not know English. Therefore I have no way of communicating that I prefer this painting of nothing to that one of something.

No way to speak of my past or hopes for the future, of my glasses mysteriously shattered in Rotterdam, the statue of Eros and Psyche in the Summer Garden, the sudden, shrill cries in the streets of Sao Paulo, a watch abruptly stopping in Paris.

No way to tell the joke about the rabbi and the parrot, the bartender and the duck, the Pope and porte-cochere.

You will understand why you have received no letters from me and why yours have gone unread.

用手臂或双臂搂着你，轻柔地施压
吗；我可以直接亲你的嘴唇吗；先亲
你脖子左侧的韧带；然后亲你的两个
乳头；如此等等。

我反正也无法判断她的反应。

我不懂英文。所以我无法表明
我喜欢的是这幅空无一物的画
而不是那幅上面有东西的。

无法诉说我的过去或对未来的憧憬，我的
眼镜如何在鹿特丹神秘兮兮地碎裂，
夏日花园里爱神与美女的塑像，圣保罗
街上突然的尖叫，一块手表
在巴黎忽然停掉。

无法讲犹太牧师与鹦鹉的笑话，或者
讲酒吧服务员与鸭子，或教皇与泊车点。

你应该明白为何你从未收到我的信，
为何你的信我从未打开。

Those, that is, where you write so precisely of the
confluence of the visible universe with the invisible,
and of the lens of dark matter.

No way to differentiate the hall of mirrors from the
meadow mullein, the beetlebung from the
pinkletink, the kettlehole from the ventifact.

Nor can I utter the words science, séance, silence,
language and languish.

Nor can I tell of the arboreal shadows elongated and
shifting along the wall as the sun's angle
approaches maximum hibernal declination.

Cannot tell of the almond-eyed face that peered from
the well, the ship of stone whose sail was a tongue.

And I cannot report that this rose has twenty-four
petals, one slightly cankered.

Cannot tell how I dismantled it myself at this desk.

Cannot ask the name of this rose.

我指的是你的那些信，如此准确地描述
　　可见宇宙和不可见宇宙怎样汇合
　　以及暗物质的镜头。

无法区分镜子的走廊与毛蕊的草坪，
　　甲虫树与小雨蛙，
　　锅穴与风磨石。

我也无法发这些词的音：science，séance，silence，
　　language 和 languish。

我也无法描述当太阳的斜度靠近冬令最低点时，树木
　　的影子顺着墙壁延伸移动。

无法描述杏仁眼的面孔从井底
　　向外窥探，石船以舌头为帆。

我无法报告这朵玫瑰有二十四片花瓣，
　　其中一片微有虫蛀。

无法陈述我怎样在这张桌子上一手把它掰散。

无法问这朵玫瑰的名字。

I cannot repeat the words of the Recording Angel or
those of the Angel of Erasure.

Can speak neither of things abounding nor of things
disappearing.

Still the games continue. A muscular man waves a
stick at a ball. A woman in white, arms
outstretched, carves a true circle in space. A village
turns to dust in the chalk hills.

Because I do not know English I have been variously
called Mr. Twisted, The One Undone, The
Nonrespondent, The Truly Lost Boy, and Laughed-
At-By-Horses.

The war is declared ended, almost before it has begun.

They have named it the Ultimate Combat between
Nearness and Distance.

I do not know English.

我无法重复记录天使或删除天使
　　所说的话。

无法述说比比皆是的物体，或那些消失之中的
　　东西。

然而游戏还在继续。一位健壮的男子对着球
　　挥舞棍子。一位白衣女子，两臂张开，
　　在空中
　　画一个真实的圆圈。一座村庄在粉笔山上化为灰烬。

我不懂英文，所以我有各种各样的绰号
　　别扭先生，被毁者，无反应者，
　　彻底迷失的男孩，被马讥讽的人。

战争几乎都还没开始，就已宣布结束。

他们把它命名为“近与远的决战”。

我不懂英文。

And

The ship—what was her name, its name?
Was it The Moth? Or The Moth
that Electrifies Night? Or The Moth

that Divides the Night in Half
in its Passage toward the Fire?
The fire of forgetting, that is,

as we remember it,
while in the scatter song of dailiness
as it eddies out

near turns to far, beeches, red cedars and oaks
dating to the revolution, and a few long before,
suddenly in unison are seen to fall,

for so somewhere it is writ.
And your project abandoned in fragments
there beneath the elements,

然后

那船——她的名字是什么，它的名字？
是叫飞蛾，还是震惊黑夜的
飞蛾，还是扑向

火焰，劈开黑夜的
飞蛾？
那是遗忘之火

如我们记忆中的，
在日常琐碎的歌曲里
当它随旋涡漂走

由近变远，山毛榉、红杉与橡木
革命时代种的，有些甚至更久，
突然一起倒下，

因为某处早有预言。
你的项目半途而废
碎片零散在大自然里，

the snow of the season enfolding it,
the flames of the season consuming it,
improving it: Hashish, the tales it

tells, the scented oils and modern festivals,
the sphinx-like heads and the shining ornaments
for ankle, waist, neck and wrist,

dioramas, cosmoramas, pleoramas
(from pleo, "I sail," "I go by water"),
the hierophant in wax, the iron and glass,

the artificial rain and winds,
mosaic thresholds, all of this
bathed from above in diffuse light.

We share the invisible nature of these
things, our bodies and theirs.
And the moon did not appear that night.

(to the memory of a suicide)

季节的雪包裹着它，
季节的火吞噬它，
改善它：海吸希，它讲的

故事，香油和现代节日，
狮身人面般的头，晶莹的装饰物
在脚腕、腰、脖子和手腕上，

缩微布景，全球图片，pleo 风景
(pleo，意思是“我扬帆”、“我走水路”)，
蜡制的祭司长、铁与玻璃

人造的风雨，
拼花图案的门槛，这一切
都沉浸在散漫的亮光里。

我们跟这些一样有不可见的
本质，我们的身体和它们的。
那夜月亮没有露面。

纪念某次自杀

Of

Of this photograph no one has taken

Eyes both a veil and sexual organ
The play as they always say

of light against shadow
first light then shadow then the shadow-play

Is it in color or black and white?

Yes it is in color or black and white

There are leaves drifting down,
a tiny skiff prepared to embark

across the waters of a painter's studio
toward a tower of clouds beyond the glass

The scatter of things

这

这张照片没人拍过

眼睛是面纱也是生殖器
如人们常说的，是光

与影的游戏
先光，后影，然后是影子戏

是彩色的还是黑白？

是的，是彩色或是黑白

叶子纷纷飘落，
一叶小舟准备起航

穿越画家作坊的水面
驶往玻璃之外的云塔

东西七零八碎

the room choking on pages
and the torn remnants of pages

No one to answer the telephone's ring
(Dearest Reader are there still phones still rings?)

They are afloat the two of them
in a sea of something

or perhaps they are drowning
or waiting for the wind to gather them up

into a palinode, a canticle, a stanza

If she has a question
will it go unasked?

(Are there still questions and questions unasked
Dearest Reader from the future-past?)

Berries brilliant orange on the hawthorn
this Wednesday late November

房间被书页窒息
那些书页的碎片

电话铃响也没人接
（最亲爱的读者，还有电话和铃声吗？）

他们在漂，他俩
在某种海洋里

或许他们行将溺亡
或许在等待风把他们卷起

化为一首翻案诗，赞美诗，诗章

如果她有问题
会有提问的机会吗？

（穿越时空的最亲爱的读者，
还有问题吗，还有没问的问题吗？）

山楂树的果子橘黄鲜艳
十一月底的这个星期三

Blurred wing at the edge of the frame

Eyes unfocused lost in her
thoughts as they always say

Eyes at once fixed and in motion

gilded aleph emerging from her mouth
mouth emerging from her mouth

So, it's claimed, an age begins

This photograph no one has seen
offers itself in evidence

框架边模糊的翅膀

眼神发呆，她在沉思
默想，如人们常说

眼睛同时凝视又转动

镀金的 A 从她的嘴里涌出
嘴从她的嘴里冒出

就这样，有人宣称，一个时代开始了

这张无人见过的照片
为它自己作证

The Thought

We breathe in, we do not think
of it. We walk and we speak

beneath the blue-flowering trees
and do not think. We breathe.

We cross the stone bridge
above a fisherman in a skiff.

We pass the blind man, the legless man
and the woman who sings of a coming storm.

We sit by the river in the rising wind,
we raised the crazed cup to our lips

and do not think,
here where the light does not differ from dark,

here where pages tumble to the floor,
here in the lake of ink, the stain of ink

思想

我们吸气，我们不去想
它。我们走路，我们

在开满蓝花的树下聊天
也不去想它。我们呼吸。

我们跨过石桥
桥下一个渔人划着小舟。

我们路经盲人、无腿人
和歌唱风雨欲来的女人。

我们在起风时坐在河畔，
我们举起裂纹式的杯子到唇边

也不去想它，
此处光明与黑暗并无区分，

此处书页滚落到地板上，
此处在墨水湖里，墨水的痕迹中

where we fashion a calendar from a wall.

Invisible lake, unreachable shore.

Exhale and do not think.

Close their eyes a final time close our eyes.

(to Faraj Bayrakdar)

我们从墙上画出一张日历。

看不见的湖，不可及的岸。

呼气，不要想。

闭上他们的眼睛，最后一次，闭上我们的眼睛。

献给法拉吉·贝拉克达尔

Untitled (February 2000)

The naked woman at the window
her back to you, bowing the violin

behind the lace curtain
directly above the street

is not a fiction
as the partita is not a fiction

its theme and variations
ornaments and fills

not a fiction
as the one-way street still

wet from all this
rain is no fiction

and nakedness not a fiction.
It reads us like a book

无题（2000 年 2 月）

窗户边裸体的女人
背冲着你，拉着小提琴

在绣花窗帘后
街道的正上面

这不是虚构
正如组曲不是虚构

它的主题和变奏
装饰音和填补符

不是虚构
正如这雨后

依然湿漉漉的单行道
不是虚构

裸体不是虚构。
它对我们了如指掌

as we listen to its music
through milky eyes wide shut.

And what does this fiction think of us?
The rain, the notes, both softly fall.
Slight errors of intonation do not matter
in the faded green

notebooks where we record these
things, and conceal other things.

What's the name of that tree, anyway,
with yellow flowers, small silver leaves,

planted in the concrete—
I used to know.

As for today, Leap Year Day,
the window was empty.

当我们透过模糊、紧闭的
眼睛聆听它的音乐。

这虚构如何看待我们呢？
雨点，音符，都悄悄地坠落。
音调上的小差错并不要紧
在这褪色的绿本子里

我们记录这些
东西，掩盖别的。

那棵树到底叫什么，
开着黄花，长着小银叶，

种在水泥地里——
我曾经知道。

至于今天，是闰日，
窗口空空如也。

So

So the promise of happiness?
he asked a frog

then swallowed the frog
And the buzz of memory?

he asked the page
before lighting the page

And by night the sliding stars
beyond the night itself

那么

那么幸福的诺言呢？
他问一只青蛙

然后把青蛙吞掉
而记忆的嗡嗡声呢？

他问那书页
在他点燃书页之前

夜晚滑行的群星
在夜的自身之外

Crease

Crease in the snow field
of evening within us

How the owl stares
and startles there

fashioning mindless elegy
So the remembered world's

songs and flooded paths
This heap of photographs

皱折

我们内心的黄昏
雪地布满皱折

猫头鹰如何大眼圆睁
在那里惊跳

炮制没头没脑的挽歌
这样，记忆中的世界

它的歌声与淹没的路
这一堆照片

This

This perfect half-moon
of lies in the capital

Crooks and fools in power what's new
and our search has begun for signs of spring

Maybe those two bluebirds
flashing past the hawthorn yesterday

Against that, the jangle of a spoon in a cup
and a child this day swept out to sea

这个

这个完美的半月
属于都市的谎言

骗子和傻瓜正当权，有什么稀奇
我们已开始寻找春天的征兆

或许那两只蓝知更鸟
昨日从山楂树间一闪而过

在那背景里，调羹敲杯的刺耳之音
此日一个小孩被大海卷走

The Dream of Narcissus

The dream of Narcissus,
that there would be a silence loud as time

The dream of the writer,
that there could be a silence loud as time

The dream of time,
that rest might come

The dream of rest,
that unrest might arise

The dream of the palm,
that pilgrims would enter the village

The dream of the village,
that they depart with their fronds

And the house dreaming of its leveling,
and the exile of his well

水仙的梦

水仙的梦，
会有一片沉寂如时间一样响亮

作者的梦，
可有一片沉寂如时间一样响亮

时间的梦，
安息将至

安息的梦，
骚乱将起

棕榈树的梦，
朝圣者将走进村庄

村庄的梦，
他们拿着棕榈叶离开

房子梦见自己被夷平，
流亡者梦见自己的水井

The dream of night,

that the day would be purified

The dream of day,

that the dark would be lifted

And the dream of the dream,

but who's to speak of this

黑夜的梦，

白昼将变得纯洁

白昼的梦，

黑暗将被揭开

而梦的梦，

又会有谁来讲

But They Have Fallen

But they have fallen to the ground
amid the twigs and leaves

all dry. And we bend
to pick them up, these things,

we think to pick them up
but we cannot

hard as we try.
It is too dark or else too light.

There's been a failure at the source of light,
a fractured moon or swollen sun,

and our fingers one by one
have grown numb.

可它们已经

可它们已经掉到地上
在枝干与落叶之间

全然干燥。我们弯腰
去捡，这些东西，

我们想要捡起来
可是不行

无论多么努力。
天太黑或是太亮。

光源那里出了故障，
破碎的月亮，或臃肿的太阳，

我们的手指已一根根地
麻木。

My Lecture

My lecture. It began in dreams,
the topics merging.

Painters and dancers,
I've forgotten your names

as you have mine.
We were there together

in that vast room,
and the rent was due.

We moved cautiously,
so as not to offend.

We spoke in the end,
sotto voce, of the gates

we must pass through
and the ruins beyond,

我的讲座

我的讲座。在梦里开始，
讲题融合在一起。

画家和舞蹈者，
我已忘了你们的名字

就如你们忘了我的。
我们曾一起

在那宽敞的房间里，
房租已经到期。

我们小心翼翼地移动，
以免冒犯别人。

最后我们说话了，
低声细语，讲到

我们必须穿过的大门
和那后面的废墟，

motion as time,

gesture as light,

the fracturing patterns,

all those fictions and fears

and the years,

rent still due.

移动作为时间，
手势作为光线，

破裂的模式，
那一切虚构与恐惧

以及岁月，
房租还是要交。

The Classical Study

I asked the Master of Shadows
wherefore and wherefrom

but he said that art was short
and life was long.

Said: let us praise
those flames that consume the day

stone by stone
and the lilac by the barn

and the hours when you were young
and the mother- and the father-tongue.

Curled by fire the leaves of grass,
buckled, the roof beam,

shattered, the wagon's haft,
ash-flecks in the wind's swell.

古典研究

我问黑影大师
何去何从

可他说，艺术短暂
生命常青。

说：让我们赞美
那些一砖一瓦地

吞噬白昼的火焰
还有谷仓边的丁香花

年轻的时光
母语和父语。

被火焰卷起的草叶，
缩成一团，栋梁

断裂，推车的把手
在强风里化为灰烬。

Have you forgotten the whistling of the stones,
the heave and shift of the windrows?

So I asked the Master of Shadows
about the above and the below,

the this and the that,
the first and the last,

but he said,
I am no master

only a shadow,
and he laughed.

难道你忘了石头的呼啸，
稻草堆起伏蜿蜒？

于是我问黑影大师
有关上与下，

这和那，
起初和最后，

可他说，
我不是大师

只是一个影子，
然后他大笑。

The Classical Study (6)

I asked the Master among
the buildings of Bricktown
where my future lay.

Eyes rolling up, he replied,
Your fate is the same
as the buildings of Bricktown,

the children, the streets,
the stray dogs of Bricktown,
the spike-heeled whores

and slim hustlers of Bricktown.
Your words are the same
as those spoken and sung

by the citizens of Bricktown.
The sundry sights you see
you see through the windows

古典研究（六）

我问大师
在砖头镇的楼房间
我的未来属于哪里。

他眼珠滴溜一转，回答
你的命运
跟砖头镇的楼房，

砖头镇的孩子们，
街道，野狗，
还有砖头镇穿高跟鞋的妓女

以及精瘦的骗子一样。
你讲的话
跟砖头镇居民

说唱的一样。
你看到的五花八门的场景
你是透过砖头镇的窗户

and doorways of Bricktown,
among the alleys of Bricktown,
by the river's ruined shore

wending through Bricktown.
Don't search for your face in that tide
or for a skiff to ferry you out to sea.

Memorize its streets
and study its walls.
One severed song fits all.

和门道,

在砖头镇的小巷里,

在那穿过砖头镇的河流

荒芜的岸边看到的。

不要在那潮水里寻找你的面孔

也不要找一叶小舟渡你过海。

记住它的街道

研究它的墙壁。

一首断裂的歌适合一切。

L'Azur

I returned a book to John Ashbery last week. It was 1" ×1" ×1", a perfect cube. "Gee, Michael, you've had that book for twelve years. What took you so long?" "It was surprisingly dense," I answered, "almost as if nine-tenths of the universe's dark matter were packed inside. Also, that azure cover put me off for a good while. I thought it might be a Symbolist work, something about swans and ice, and you know how I've detested swans ever since that incident ..." "Did she ever recover?" asked John. "Outwardly she's fine, but, really, she's never been the same." "Well, I'm not entirely myself today either," said John, "but I'm happy to have that book back. I've always liked that strange title. What do you think it means?"

湛蓝

上星期我把一本书还给约翰·阿什伯利。那书是一个完美的立体方块，1×1×1 英寸。“天哪，迈克尔，这本书你借了十二年。怎么这么久不还？”“因为它出奇地深奥，”我回答，“仿佛里面聚集了整个宇宙十分之九的暗物质。而且，那湛蓝的封面让我反感了好一阵子。我想那可能是象征派的作品，有关天鹅与冰雪，你知道自从那件事以后，我是多么憎恶天鹅……”“她后来康复了吗？”约翰问。“外表看来她是好了，不过，说真的，她跟从前不一样了。”“嗯，我今天也有点不舒服，”约翰说，“不过我很高兴这书还回来了。我一向喜欢那古怪的书名。你说它是什么意思？”

What I Did Not Say

What I did not say was that within this tiny book, this 1"×1"×1" cube, there was but one word. It was not even an unusual word, rather one people once used all the time as a call or a greeting, mornings or evenings, or else to express a certain delight, for example in the color of a lover's eyes or the grace of his or her form. A word, then, with no specific referent or single meaning, one often simply meant to intimate concord or mutual understanding, agreement or solidarity. This word had been banned from public utterance for many years, but it had subsequently, as often happens, worked its way back into common parlance until the point where the ban itself became a subject of ridicule, and those who had imposed the ban were reviled, where formerly they had been cheered and celebrated. Is it possible to conceive that this almost invisible book, with that one word in it, may have been responsible for this turn of affairs?

我没说的

我没说的是，在这本小书，这块 1×1×1 的方块里，只有一个字。它甚至不是什么僻字生词，而是一个人们过去常用来早晚打招呼或问候的字，或用来表达某种喜悦，比如，对情人眼睛的颜色或其体形之优雅而生的欣喜。就是说，这是一个没有具体所指或单独意义的字，一个仅用来表示和谐或同感，一致或团结的字。这个字在大众语言里已禁用多年了，但是正如常常发生的，它最终又回到通用语里，直到有一天禁令本身成了被嘲笑的对象。而那些强行禁令的人，过去曾受众人拥戴，现在则成过街老鼠。能否想象，这本微不足道、只含那一个字的小书，有可能是这一切变化的起因？

Move

Move that barn a little to the left
if you would

and that memory of a barn
a little to the right

until they coincide.
That's good.

移动

若你愿意
把那谷仓稍往左移

把那谷仓的回忆
稍往右移

直到两者巧合。
那样刚好。

Gu Cheng

Nobody wishes for the name
of the nameless flower.

Nobody wants to hear
the untellable tale.

No one wants you to return
as the skeleton of a nameless bird

bright plumage shed
on its flight toward death.

Who cares to drink
from the overturned pail of hours

spreading its red stain
across the millet fields?

顾城

没人想要
无名小花的名字。[1]

没人想听
无法讲述的故事。

没人想你归来
作为一只无名鸟的骸骨

灿烂的羽衣脱落在
冲向死亡的途中。

谁会去喝
打翻的时光之杯的水

红色斑迹
撒满粟田？

1 顾城写过一首诗，题为《无名的小花》。

Who would turn the pages
of the one book, the unreadable book,

as curtains tremble in the early
breeze? Earth bearing us in circles,

bearing the hovels and palaces,
night herons and night jasmine,

the wave-skimmers, the dancers,
the lovers intertwined, the

tiny blossoms and toxic piles,
clocktowers and sentinel fires,

whirled round and round,
the caws and cries.

谁会翻开
那本书，那本不可读的书

当帘幕在晨风中
颤抖？地球带着我们转圈，

带着茅舍与宫殿，
夜鹭与夜来香，

带着戏浪者，舞蹈者，
缠绕相拥的情人，

小花与废物堆，
钟楼与哨兵的火把，

旋转一圈又一圈，
鸦鸣鸟泣。

Bees (6/12/06)

What the poem knows
I know not

What the pen writes
I do not

What the page says
I cannot hear

in this din, this din,
this summoning, spiral

din, without with-
in, this call, this hum

of bees among
the hawthorn's bright

mays today this
noise this day

蜂群 (2006 年 6 月 12 日)

诗知道的

我不知

笔写的

我没写

书页说的

我听不见

在这喧嚣，这喧嚣，

这召唤，螺旋的

喧嚣里，里里，外

外，这召唤，这蜂群的

嗡嗡之音，在

山楂鲜艳的

花朵间今天这

噪声这默默

of silent suicides
in ink-dark light

far off, far away
And one to one

to conjure none
Add us to them,

impossible sum
of wind and sand,

chance and plan,
this din, this hum

of day turned night
and green undone

自杀的日子
在遥远的天边

墨黑之光里
一加一

变成零
我们加他们，

总和不可能
就像风加沙，

机遇加计划，
这喧嚣，这白昼

变成黑夜，绿色变成
死亡的嗡嗡之音

From "Thread" (1)

From the Mercury Fountain, Mahmoud,

spills a stream

echo of things

sun to stone speaking

cicada to poppy

not milk of paradise

no river of stars in the dark

just the bent wheel of days

meaningless ripples in the heat

线条 (1)

从汞泉中，玛姆德[1]，
涌出一条小溪
万物的回声
太阳跟石头说话
蝉跟罂粟花
不是天堂的牛奶
没有黑暗里的星河
只是时光破瘪的轮子
热气中无意义的涟漪

1　指巴勒斯坦著名诗人玛姆德 · 达尔维西 (Mahmoud Darwish, 1941—2008)。

From "Thread" (2)

It is the role of the lovers to set fire to the book.

In the palm garden at night they set fire to the book

and read by the light of the book.

Syllables, particles of glass, they pass back and forth
in the dark.

The two, invisible—transparent—in the book,

their voices muffled by the book.

It is the role of the lovers to be figures of the book,

the illegible book,

changing as the pages turn,

now joined, now clawing the fruit from each other's
limbs,

线条 (2)

恋爱中的人，他们的责任是焚书。

黑夜里，在棕榈园，他们放火烧书

借着火光阅读。

音节，玻璃碎片，他们在黑暗中来回传递。

他俩，隐形——透明——在书里，

声音被书压抑。

恋爱中的人，他们的责任是扮演书的角色，

那字迹模糊的书，

随着书页的翻动而变化，

有时两体合一，有时从彼此四肢上挖取果子，

now interlaced, now tearing at throat and vein,

then splayfoot, then winged, then ember,

as the music of the book,

rustling through the palms,

instructs.

有时交织缠绕，有时撕破彼此的喉咙与血管，

一会儿是八字脚，一会儿插翅高飞，一会儿化为灰烬，

当书的音乐，

在棕榈树间窸窣作响，

谆谆教诲。

迈克·帕尔玛创作年表简编

黄运特　编译

1943 年　5 月 11 日出生在纽约市。

1961 年　进哈佛大学，主修法国历史与文学专业。

1963 年　参加温哥华诗歌大会，一次对北美诗歌具有重大影响的聚会。

1964—1965 年　与克拉克·库利奇合办《魔术家》(*Joglars*) 诗歌杂志。

1965 年　哈佛大学本科毕业。

1965—1966 年　为了反抗美国越战，躲避征兵，移居欧洲一年，不断被美国政府追踪。

1967—1968 年　攻读哈佛大学比较文学硕士学位，1968 年毕业。

1968—1969 年　任哈佛大学讲师。

1969 年　移居旧金山。

1970—1972 年　任圣何塞州立学院讲师。

1971 年 处女诗集《O 城市的计划》(*Plan of the City of O*) 由谷仓梦社出版。

1972 年 11 月 24 日，与卡西·西蒙结婚。诗集《布莱克的牛顿》(*Blake's Newton*) 由黑麻雀社出版。与舞蹈家玛格丽特·詹金斯合作舞剧《干扰》(*Interferences*)，从此至今，跟詹金斯舞蹈团合作过二十几次。

1973 年 诗集《C 的歌》(*C's Songs*) 由沙美元社出版。

1974 年 诗集《圆门》(*The Circular Gates*) 由黑麻雀社出版。

1975 年 获美国国家艺术基金会诗歌奖金。

1977 年 4 月 28 日，女儿萨拉出生。诗集《无音乐》(*Without Music*) 由黑麻雀社出版。

1980 年 诗集《镜子的透明度》(*Transparency of the Mirror*) 由小恐龙社出版。翻译法国诗人兰波的著作《元音》。诗集《狂魂》(*Alogon*) 由敦巴社出版。

1981 年 诗集《回音湖札记》(*Notes for Echo Lake*) 由北边社出版。

1982 年 再次获得美国国家艺术基金会诗歌奖金。

1983 年 编辑《信号的密码：诗论新作》(*Code of Signals: Recent Writings in Poetics*)，由北大西洋社出版。

1984 年 诗集《第一个图像》(*First Figure*) 由北边社出版。

1986 年 任艾奥瓦大学创作系客座诗人。

1987 年 诗作《献给萨拉的歌》(*Song for Sarah*)，画家欧文·佩特林配图，由龙虾湾社出版。

1988 年 诗集《太阳》(*Sun*) 由北边社出版。诗作《为一次朗诵》(*For a Reading*) 由迪亚艺术基金会出版。

1989 年 《太阳》荣获西部笔会诗歌奖。

1989—1990 年 获古根海姆诗歌奖。

1990 年 与诗人诺玛·科尔合译《超现实主义者看艺术》。《太阳》法文译本出版。

1992 年 翻译法国诗人伊曼纽尔·霍卡德的《桌子的理论》。《回音湖札记》法文译本出版。参加巴黎诗歌朗诵会。

1992—1994 年 主持里拉·华莱士读者文摘基金会作家奖。

1993 年 诗集《地下的字母表》(*An Alphabet Underground*) 译成丹麦语，在哥本哈根出版。

1994 年 翻译俄国诗人亚历克塞·帕希科夫的《胆矾》。参加布拉格诗歌朗诵会。与詹金斯舞蹈团一起巡游欧洲。

1995 年 诗集《在通道》(*At Passages*) 由北点社出版。《在通道》获美国诗歌奖。参加美国国会图书馆诗歌朗诵会。

1996 年 翻译霍卡德的《三个伦理故事》。《在通道》法文译本出版。

1997 年 译编《太阳能解释一切：当代巴西诗人二十家》(*Nothing the Sun Could Not Explain: 20 Contemporary Brazilian Poets*)，由日月社出版。参加鹿特丹国际诗歌会。

1998 年 诗集《狮子桥：1972—1995 年诗选》(*The Lion Bridge: Selected Poetry 1972—1995*) 由新方向社出版。

1999 年　诗集《丹麦笔记本》(*The Danish Notebook*) 由 Avec 社出版。坦普尔大学驻校作家。

1999—2004 年　任美国诗歌学院院长。

2000 年　诗集《玻璃的承诺》(*Promises of Glass*) 由新方向社出版。《太阳》俄文译本出版。参加第一届柏林国际文学节。

2001 年　诗集《密码显现：1977—1988 年诗选》(*Codes Appearing: Poems 1977—1988*) 由新方向社出版。获美国诗歌协会雪莱纪念奖。

2002 年　任那洛巴大学客座诗歌教授。

2002—2003 年　任英国加迪夫大学客座诗歌教授。

2003 年　《太阳能解释一切》再版。《太阳》瑞典语译本出版。圣玛丽学院杰出客座诗人。与北岛等诗人一起参加贝洛伊特学院国际诗歌节。密歇根大学驻校诗人。在巴黎、华盛顿、旧金山、芝加哥等地举办诗歌朗诵会。

2004 年　日语译本《微粒玫瑰》(*The Particle Rose*) 在东京出版。在耶鲁大学、史密斯学院等地举办诗歌朗诵会。

2005 年　诗集《飞蛾伴侣》(*Company of Moths*) 由新方向社出版。参加柏林国际文学节。

2006 年　获美国诗人学会华莱士·史蒂文斯诗歌奖。圣玛丽学院杰出客座诗人。芝加哥大学客座教授。在圣母大学与北岛一起诗歌朗诵。

2007 年　诗选《反天空》被译成日语出版。加利福尼亚艺术学院驻校诗人。参加布朗大学波德莱尔大会。参加东京诗歌与舞蹈节。在旧金山州立大学作乔治·奥本纪念报告。

2008 年　散文集《活动的界限：散文与报告选集》(*Active Boundaries: Selected Essays and Talks*) 由新方向社出版。华盛顿大学驻校诗人。新西兰维多利亚大学驻校诗人。在俄克拉荷马大学、艾奥瓦作家坊、韦斯利安大学等地举办诗歌朗诵会。

2009 年　诗集《艾吉循环》(*Aygi Cycle*) 被译成比利时语出版。在旧金山、纽约、伊斯坦布尔等地举办诗歌朗诵会。

2010 年　参加悉尼作家节和鹿特丹国际诗歌节。在芝加哥、亚利桑那、斯坦福大学、洛杉矶、纽约等地作诗歌朗诵和报告。

2011年 诗集《线条》(*Thread*) 由新方向社出版。诗选《对日照》(*Gegenschein*) 被译成德语，在柏林出版。诗选《疯子与扫把》(*Madman with Broom*) 被译成中文，由牛津大学出版社出版。